PATCHWORK  & other Quilting

By LINDA S. WEEKS

**LITTLE
CRAFT BOOK
SERIES**

**STERLING
PUBLISHING CO., INC. NEW YORK**
Oak Tree Press Co., Ltd.
London & Sydney
SAUNDERS OF TORONTO, Ltd., Don Mills, Canada

Little Craft Book Series

The author would like to thank the following people from Tennessee for contributing quilts for this book: Mrs. Annie Stanley of Woodville; Mrs. Lucille Lane of Woodville; Mrs. Parks (Mama Goldie) of Nutbush; Dana Parks of Nutbush; Mrs. Russell Jackocks of Woodville and Lou Ann Camp of Halls.

Photographs by Bob Weeks
Drawings by Nancy Hom

Copyright © 1973 by Sterling Publishing Co., Inc.
419 Park Avenue South, New York, N.Y. 10016
Distributed in Canada by Saunders of Toronto, Ltd., Don Mills, Ontario
British edition published by Oak Tree Press Co., Ltd., Nassau, Bahamas
Distributed in Australia and New Zealand by Oak Tree Press Co., Ltd.,
P.O. Box 34, Brickfield Hill, Sydney 2000, N.S.W.
Distributed in the United Kingdom and elsewhere in the British Commonwealth
by Ward Lock Ltd., 116 Baker Street, London W 1
Manufactured in the United States of America
All rights reserved
Library of Congress Catalog Card No.: 73-83452
ISBN 0-8069-5290-3   UK 7061-2465-0
5291-1

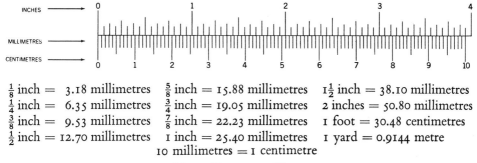

$\frac{1}{8}$ inch = 3.18 millimetres	$\frac{5}{8}$ inch = 15.88 millimetres	$1\frac{1}{2}$ inch = 38.10 millimetres
$\frac{1}{4}$ inch = 6.35 millimetres	$\frac{3}{4}$ inch = 19.05 millimetres	2 inches = 50.80 millimetres
$\frac{3}{8}$ inch = 9.53 millimetres	$\frac{7}{8}$ inch = 22.23 millimetres	1 foot = 30.48 centimetres
$\frac{1}{2}$ inch = 12.70 millimetres	1 inch = 25.40 millimetres	1 yard = 0.9144 metre

10 millimetres = 1 centimetre

Metric Conversion Chart

Contents

Before You Begin

Whoever said that quilting is only for people with lots of time to spare could not have been more wrong. Quilting is for everyone—young and old, men and women, career girls and housewives. Any quilt that *you* design and quilt is something to treasure and be proud of. Do not let the opportunity to make your own hand-made quilt pass because you feel harried or do not know how to start. Making a quilt requires only basic sewing skills, yet the finished product is satisfying and beautiful and certainly original.

Quilting is a two-part process. First you choose a top piece or a pattern, which you can design and piece together according to the instructions in this book. Then you quilt the designed part to another piece of material, with a layer of filling in between. The pattern of the quilting stitches is as important a part of your quilt as is the design itself.

To get the feel of quilting, thumb through this book and look at the different patterns. Better yet, if there is someone you know who owns some quilts, take a look at a real quilt, not just a picture, and see what it feels like and how beautiful the stitchery can be. When you decide on a pattern, start looking for the right material or rummage through sewing scraps and pick out pieces of material with special meaning. Because each quilt is hand-made, you add your personal touch to any pattern, and the result, of course, is a very personal quilt. For example, you can alter the Lone Star on page 23 in hundreds of ways by simply changing the combination of colors in making the star.

If you need a reason to begin, other than for the pleasure of making your own quilt, think of giving a quilt the next time you need a special present for a new bride or a new family addition. Generations ago, American girls were not only expected to have completed a number of quilts for their own home linens before marrying, but women and friends of the community got together and quilted a bridal or wedding quilt for the new bride. Often, showers were given for the bride, and each guest brought a quilt block, which the bride put together and then invited the guests to a quilting bee. Also, any new mother would be proud to have a special baby quilt for her newborn—and there is a special section in this book on baby and infant quilts.

Most experienced quilters are only too glad to help a novice. If you have any questions, they would probably be glad to help. In fact, why not consider the revival of the community quilting bee?

Materials

Materials for quilting are inexpensive and readily available in most homes. The only item a new quilter might have to purchase is a quilting frame and even this is easy to construct if you are at all talented with a saw and drill. See Illus. 1 for a do-it-yourself frame. Purchase what is called 1 × 2 inch lumber and cut it to your size specifications (see page 16 for instructions on determining your quilt size). Cut two strips the length you want your longest quilt, and two

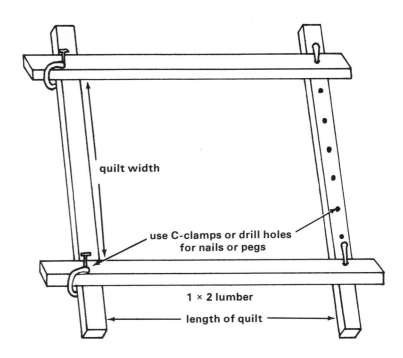

quilt width

use C-clamps or drill holes for nails or pegs

1 × 2 lumber

length of quilt

strips to equal the quilt width (plus an extra 6 inches for tacking room). Drill holes at 2- or 3-inch intervals if you plan to use nails or pegs to hold the quilt frame intact, or eliminate the drilling and use C-clamps, as shown.

It is a good idea to organize a quilting box in which you can keep several needles of the same size, some adhesive tape to protect your fingertips from needle pricks, and a couple of thimbles. If you are not accustomed to wearing a thimble,

now is the time to learn, for it is almost impossible to quilt without one.

Most quilters recommend using a short, sharp needle (No. 8 or 9) for quilting and a longer needle for piecing tops. When you have completed your first quilt, you will notice that your needle has developed a slight curvature and is easier to use. With this initiation completed, your needle is an official quilting needle. Some quilters think needles should be sold with a curvature, but

5

purists believe each hand must break in its own needle.

In the past, Number 30 quilting thread was always used for the quilting stitch, but today many quilters prefer to use a 40 or 50 thread, as it makes a finer stitch. The new polyester threads are much more durable than their earlier equivalents, and there is little problem with this new thread breaking easily. Always be on guard, however, for a faulty spool of thread. If your thread has a tendency to break easily, get a new spool. The color thread you use depends on your own quilt and personal taste.

In addition to the tools for quilting, you need to buy batting or filling for each quilt. This is, as its name implies, the middle layer or filling in the quilt. Until recently, quilters used cotton batting exclusively. Before processed batting was available, they even made their own batting from samples from local cotton gins. Now, however, there are several excellent synthetic blend fillings on the market. The new fillings seem to launder better than the cotton ones, because they are lighter and fluffier. Some people still prefer cotton batting, however, and if you decide to use the cotton be sure to purchase white cotton—and not the brown variety—in a single roll. These batting rolls are available in various sizes so check the measurements on the package to be sure the roll will fit your quilt.

Before you can use all these materials, you must have a quilt to quilt.

A Simple Quilt

A quilt is composed of three layers—a top, which is usually pieced or patterned in some way, the batting or filler, and the backing, also called the lining. Quilting is the process of holding these three layers of material together. The quilt backing must be cut or pieced to equal the dimensions of the quilt top. This backing should be the same type material as the quilt top and can be any color or print, although it should match or complement the quilt top. Fine white muslin or cotton is often used for backing material because it is easy to quilt, inexpensive, and looks quite nice when finished.

To become acquainted with the quilting process, buy two permanent press sheets or two pieces of permanent press material, perhaps a print for the top piece and a matching or complementary solid for the backing. Do not concern yourself yet with intricate patchwork or appliqué patterns. Instead, concentrate first on learning how to prepare your layers for quilting and then on doing the actual quilting. You can dream up and design original patterns and designs when you are familiar with what quilting itself is.

Stretching the Quilt in the Frame

To place your quilt in the frame, first thumbtack one side of the backing to the frame, spacing the thumbtacks about 3 inches apart. Gently pull the material across the frame and tack the other side. Do not worry about pulling the material taut at this time. When you have tacked the two sides onto the frame, tack the ends in the same manner.

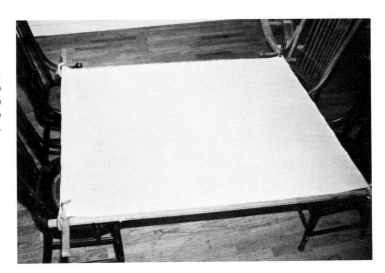

After all four sides are tacked in place, have someone help you loosen the C-clamps on two corners and pull the frame out, thereby stretching and tightening the backing. Do not pull the frames too tight, or you will tear the material.

With the backing in place, you can smooth the batting over it. Be careful not to pull holes in the batting when you unroll and stretch it. To stretch the batting over the back, slide your hand under it and gently smooth it outward. Always leave

Illus. 3. Once the backing is in
place, smooth batting over it,
leaving several inches of the
backing uncovered.

Illus. 4. When the batting is smooth, carefully place the top so it completely covers the batting.

several inches on each side of the backing free for the quilt hem.

Make sure your batting is smooth and wrinkle free, then spread the top over it. The top should completely cover the batting. When all three layers are in place, baste them together along all four sides.

If you are using a quilting hoop and not a frame,

Illus. 5. Baste all three layers in place.

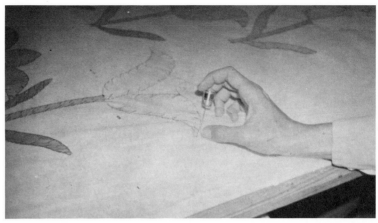

Illus. 6. Your hands should be in this position while you quilt.

follow the same directions, but instead of tacking the quilt into the frame, lay it out on the floor or a table and place all three layers together. Baste the three layers together along all four sides but place additional basting lines through the middle of the quilt to avoid wrinkles when you change the position of the hoop.

Quilting Stitch

Finally, you are ready to quilt. The actual quilting is the most time-consuming of all the steps in making a quilt, but, with a little practice, quilting becomes easy and relaxing. The purpose of quilting is to hold the three layers of the quilt together, and only as early quilters became more concerned with the beauty of their craft did they perfect the beautiful quilting designs we have today.

You do, indeed, plan the quilting pattern with the top pattern of the quilt in mind, as the secondary purpose of the quilting stitch is to enhance the design in the fabric or the pieced or appliquéd pattern you have worked so hard to make. It is recommended, therefore, that you emphasize quilting in plain areas and play down quilting stitches in patterned areas.

Most quilt top patterns will, by their design, dictate where you should quilt. You have, however, much liberty in choosing patterns for borders and strips, but keep in mind the type of quilt top pattern you have for the over-all quilt top. A geometric border might look out of place with a dainty appliqué top and a scroll border will not match a bold geometric quilt top. As with materials, keep like designs together.

If you choose an elaborate pattern, sketch the entire design onto the quilt with pencil or marking chalk before you begin quilting. Some quilting companies even sell pattern perforations in which you rub over the cut patterns with chalk dust. Always use a material for marking that will wash off easily.

The quilting stitch is a very fine running stitch. By holding your needle at an acute angle, you can punch it down and then back up near the same point. When you are experienced with this stitch, you can take several stitches on the needle before pulling the thread through the quilt. A good measure is to make 5 to 9 stitches per inch, depending on the thickness of the quilt. Try to achieve uniform stitches rather than small stitches at first.

To begin quilting, knot the end of the thread you have chosen (see page 6). Bring the needle up through the quilt and pull the knot through the backing so it is embedded in the filling or batting. This eliminates unsightly knots on the quilt back. To end off your stitch, make a simple backstitch and run the thread through the filling.

As the quilting progresses in the framed method, remove the thumbtacks and roll the quilt up gradually. As you quilt each section with the hoop, you gradually move out towards the quilt edges.

You may quilt on a sewing machine if you do not have time or space to set up a frame or if you are interested in making a lovely quilt not of a hand-made quality. Machine-quilt with a straight stitch, and a stitch length between 6 and 12 per inch. Adjust the tension according to the thickness before sewing the actual quilt. Machine-quilting yields a uniform stitch and makes quilting possible for many people who would never before have tried it.

Illus. 7. Close-up of the quilting stitch.

Finishing the Edges

When you have completed the quilting, remove the quilt from the frame. Depending on the quilt's pattern and style, there are several ways in which you can finish it. The most common method is to fold the backing over the top about 1 inch, turn it under and slip stitch it down. This simple method makes a nice finished edge that holds up well. If

Illus. 8. Cut strips of binding the length of the quilt ends plus twice the width of the binding.

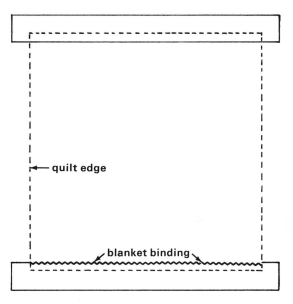

you hem by hand, use a single thread and make the stitches as invisible as possible. If the backing is a print that would not make an attractive small border on the quilt, you can roll a small piece of the front border to the quilt back and stitch it down in the same manner.

Another possible edge for a quilt is blanket binding, either satin or cotton, which you can sew round the edges of the quilt. Cut two strips of blanket binding, which you can buy in sewing supply shops, each one the length of the quilt ends plus twice the width of the binding itself. If the quilt is 36 inches and the binding is 3 inches, for example, cut the strips 42 inches long. Place the binding at least one inch overlapping the quilt edge and zig-zag stitch (see Illus. 8).

Now cut binding for the quilt sides, measuring the binding for each side the length of the quilt plus twice the width of the binding. Zig-zag stitch this length of binding in place, leaving the ends covering the width binding free (see Illus. 9).

Cut the strips you have just sewn on the quilt sides on a diagonal at the ends, giving the binding a mitered effect. Turn the cut edges under and zig-zag stitch securely (see Illus. 10).

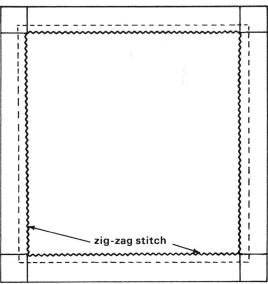

Illus. 9. Cut binding for the sides. Then zig-zag stitch the binding as shown.

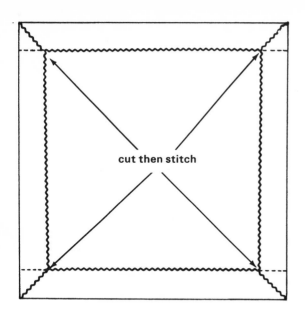

cut then stitch

Illus. 10. Cut the strips at the corners you have left open. Then zig-zag stitch them in place.

For a more elaborate edging or if you plan to use the quilt as a coverlet on a bed top, you can sew ruffles or fringe round the edge.

Some quilts require bias tape or quilt binding to finish the edges. One pattern that often requires such finishing is the flower garden quilt (see page 29), because the edge is scalloped. It is simpler and neater to sew quilt binding or bias tape onto such scalloped edges. You can, however, use bias tape, particularly colored bias tape, to create a contrast, on the edges of any quilt.

Baby quilts have a special finished look if you add satin blanket binding round the edges. Also, ruffles often decorate these small quilts nicely.

The final choice of an edging is up to you, but remember to keep the quilt material in mind when you choose the edging material.

Now that you are familiar with how to quilt, you are ready to begin designing your own quilt tops. Because the process of quilting—setting up the frame, tacking the layers to the frame, drawing on a quilting pattern and stitching—is usually more or less the same, the rest of this book will mostly be concerned with actual quilt patterns. It is taken for granted that after you design and piece the quilt top, you will choose an appropriate backing, stretch and tack it and the other two layers to the frame, quilt it, and attractively finish off the edges.

The Art of Patchwork

Patchwork quilts have been known since American colonial women stitched scraps of used clothing into bedcovers and filled them with grasses and corn husks. These early quilts were not held together with the beautiful quilting stitch we know today, but rather were tied at intervals with twine. Colonial life afforded some leisure time, and the women took pride in the making of quilts. Although quilters were forced to use small scraps of material, making new patterns became a challenge and women took pleasure in inventing patchwork designs. They developed lovely quilting patterns to decorate their patchwork or pieced tops and to hold them together. Cotton was used as a filler for the quilts.

If you hear names such as Turkey Tracks,

Illus. 11. This is only one of innumerable patchwork designs that you can create. Choose a specific pattern, or sew your patches in any decorative, abstract fashion.

Illus. 12. A nine-patch pattern.

Illus. 13. A variation of the nine-patch pattern.

Bluebirds for Happiness, Philadelphia Pavements, Jacob's Ladder or Hole in the Barn Door, you can guess where the inspiration for many patterns comes from. Early quilters took cues from the sources around them and in many early quilts birds, animals, plants and religious themes are the most prevalent. Many years before women were allowed to vote, they showed their political bias in their needlework. Presidential elections brought forth such new pattern names as Washington's Quilt, Lincoln's Platform, Jackson's Star and Democrat Rose.

Many popular patterns are known by several different names and a new member of a quilting circle might be easily confused. There are several

reasons for this name problem: If a quilt was brought into a new area with a name that someone had already used, the first name was simply dropped and a new name picked. Or, perhaps a quilter took a new pattern home with her after visiting another area and simply forgot the original name, so she just re-named the pattern. In some cases, names were mispronounced or misunderstood as the pattern travelled from area to area and a new name was born.

Today's quilter has literally hundreds of patterns to choose from when making a quilt. However, for the beginning quilter, one of the simpler patterns, like a four-patch or nine-patch would be a good start. As you gain skill in your piecing and

Illus. 14. For your first quilt, try a simple four-patch pattern, which is not difficult and is very attractive.

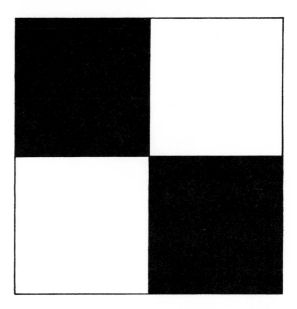

quilting ability, you can select a more complicated pattern.

A patchwork or pieced quilt is made by cutting small squares, triangles, hexagons or diamonds— first from a cardboard or sandpaper pattern and then from fabric—and piecing them together to form a large block or an over-all design. The main feature of the patchwork quilt is not the pattern but rather the colors that make up the pattern. Early quilters had an excellent eye for color and many old quilts are now on display in museums for their designs painted with needle and thread. Even a simple four-patch quilt can be beautiful if you carefully plan color combinations. As a rule of thumb for color selection, before sewing a quilt together, lay it out to see how the colors react to and complement each other.

A well made quilt is a thing of beauty, but it must also be durable. *Always* use new material— this is the most important thing to remember in piecing a quilt. The material can be sewing scraps or fabric you purchase especially for quilt pieces. It is always a good idea to test the fabric by washing and ironing a small piece before you cut out the quilt pieces. If the sample piece fades or shrinks, it is better to pre-shrink all the material rather than ruin the entire quilt. Keep in mind as you select the material the type of quilt you are making and the use the quilt will receive. Cotton, linen, fine muslin, corduroy and the new cotton blends are excellent material choices, especially since you can launder the finished quilt at home.

Square-Patch Quilts

The simple four-patch pattern is an excellent starter quilt. This pattern is made up of four squares of two contrasting colors which together form a larger block. As many blocks as necessary for any specific bed size make up the entire quilt top. To determine the quilt size, measure the bed for which you are making your quilt to get the exact size. The quilt should cover the mattress top and hang over as far as you like. If you plan to use the quilt as a blanket, allow extra room on the sides to cover a sleeping person. Allow 17 inches, or more, if the quilt is to cover the pillows on the bed, in addition to extra yardage for the foot of the bed. (See Illus. 15.)

The size of your individual squares depends on the over-all size of your quilt, but a 4-inch square

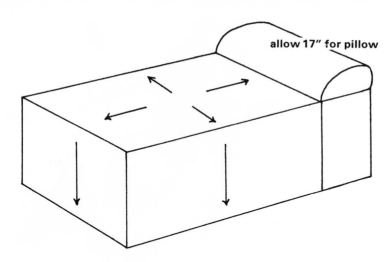

allow 17″ for pillow

Illus. 15. To determine the size to make your quilt, measure all dimensions of the bed. Add extra for a person, if you are making a blanket, or the pillow, if you are making a bedspread.

is a good size with which to begin working. Blocks smaller than 4 inches are difficult to work with and those larger than 5 or 6 inches become unwieldy for the beginner. When you decide on the block size, enlarge it $\frac{1}{2}$ inch to allow for seams, then cut several squares from cardboard or sandpaper. (For example, for a finished block that is 4 inches, cut patterns $4\frac{1}{2}$ inches.) Press all material you will use to eliminate wrinkles, then lay the cardboard pattern on the material and trace round it with a pencil or marking chalk. Be sure the pattern follows the grain of the material. Since cutting is one of the most important steps in making a quilt, use sharp scissors and trace your pattern carefully. When all your patches are cut, divide them according to color or design and either string them together with a single thread through the center, or keep them in a small, convenient box.

Since this particular pattern is usually made from scrap material, no yardage requirements are given. However, if, for example, you want a finished quilt 60 × 72 inches, you divide your 4-inch blocks into 60 and 72 and determine that you need a total of 15 blocks across and 18 blocks lengthwise. Since these blocks are in sets of two's, you divide 2 units into 18 and find that you need 9 sets down. When you divide 2 units into 15, you find that you need $7\frac{1}{2}$ units across. Ignore the $\frac{1}{2}$ unit for now, and work with 7 across. You can make up the 4 inches short of 60 on the sides when you hem the quilt. You will have a finished quilt of 56 (7 sets × 2 units × 4 inches) × 72 (9 sets × 2 units × 4 inches). Cut a total of 252 (14 × 18), $4\frac{1}{2}$-inch squares for this particular quilt.

A good color combination to keep in mind for the four-patch quilt is dark and light colors together and possibly prints and solids together. Choose colors to match a specific room's décor.

You can piece a quilt at your leisure—while talking with friends, waiting at the doctor's office or when you take time out from your job, schoolwork or household chores. If you have cut all your squares beforehand, you can piece blocks gradually, then set them together after you have completed sewing. If piecing by hand, use a simple running stitch to sew pieces together, but be sure to finish off stitches by backstitching several times so the threads will not pull out. Many quilters today prefer to machine-stitch block patterns, claiming that the machine stitches hold much

Illus. 16. This baby quilt shows one of many star designs you can make. See page 23 for star instructions.

Illus. 17. This is one possible patchwork design you can follow.

better and are quicker to make. This is a personal preference depending on whether you want to sit down at a machine or quietly work on your quilt in your spare time. Whichever method you choose, simply place right sides of the material together and stitch at least a $\frac{1}{8}$-inch seam. The seam size is not as important as making sure all seams are uniform.

For the four-patch pattern, piece the blocks in halves, then sew the halves together. When you have pieced all the blocks, sew the halves together. When all the blocks have been pieced, you can sew them together for the final quilt size or

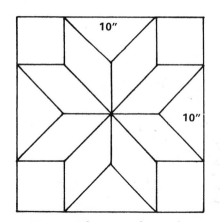

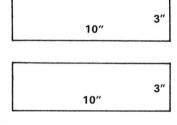

Illus. 18. Cut strips which are the length and width of your squares, and center blocks to piece at the corners.

you can set them together with strips as shown in Illus. 18 and 19. Illus. 20 is a quilt which has been joined together by strips.

Setting a quilt together in this way is not difficult. If a block is 10 inches square, for example, cut strips the same length, and whatever width you need to obtain your finished quilt size. You must also cut small center blocks the same size as the strip width (see Illus. 18). If the blocks are not square, the measurements of the strips and squares will vary accordingly.

After you have cut all the strips and squares, sew the strips to the block sides, completing one line across the quilt (see Illus. 19). When you have joined these strips and blocks, sew all the bottom blocks together as pictured in Illus. 19. Then sew these two strips together, keeping right sides together as you sew. You may edge the quilt

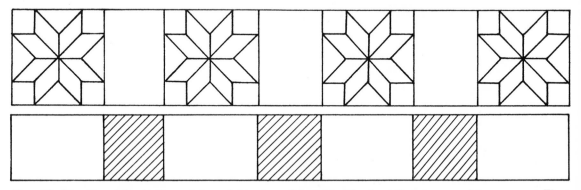

Illus. 19. Sew the strips to the patchwork blocks, with right sides together, to complete one row. Then join the strips to the center blocks for another row. Join the rows together and continue in this manner to complete the quilt top.

with a border the same width as the strips, as in Illus. 20.

If you enjoy piecing quilts but do not want to spend the time to hand-quilt them, try machine-quilting. You can do this with or without a quilting foot on the machine. The only difficulty you might have is keeping the material straight and avoiding puckers. Otherwise, tack your pieced quilt to your frame, and quilt as instructed on page 9.

If, perhaps, you do not want to hand- or machine-quilt, look around or place an ad in the local newspaper for a person who quilts. There may be someone in your area who will do extra quilting, and would be eager to quilt for you.

Illus. 20. This lovely patchwork quilt was pieced and then set together with strips as described on page 18.

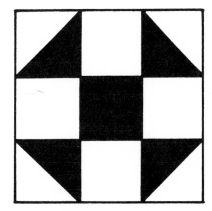

Illus. 21 (above). This simple variation of a four-patch pattern is entitled Shoofly.

Illus. 22 (right). Broken Dishes is the name of this four-patch variation.

Bow-Tie Quilt

Many interesting patchwork patterns have been developed from the basic square and one of these, with a slight variation, is the Bow-Tie or Neck-Tie Quilt, shown in Illus. 23. This quilt pattern is extremely versatile and a good example of how color combinations can change the entire look of a quilt.

The bow-tie itself is a four-square block with a small square in the middle which cuts the corners of the larger squares. Cut the middle square and two diagonal squares from the same material, thereby giving the appearance of a bow-tie. Cut the other two squares in the block from a contrasting or matched solid color or a print (see Illus. 24 for the pattern).

This quilt is simple to piece. As for the plain four-patch quilt, you can piece each bow block separately and then set all the blocks together. Since the pattern is usually pieced together from assorted material scraps, specific color combina-

Illus. 23. Patchwork designs are sometimes based round specific motifs. This pattern, as you can see, is based on a bow-tie shape.

Illus. 24. Pattern pieces for the Bow-Tie Quilt.

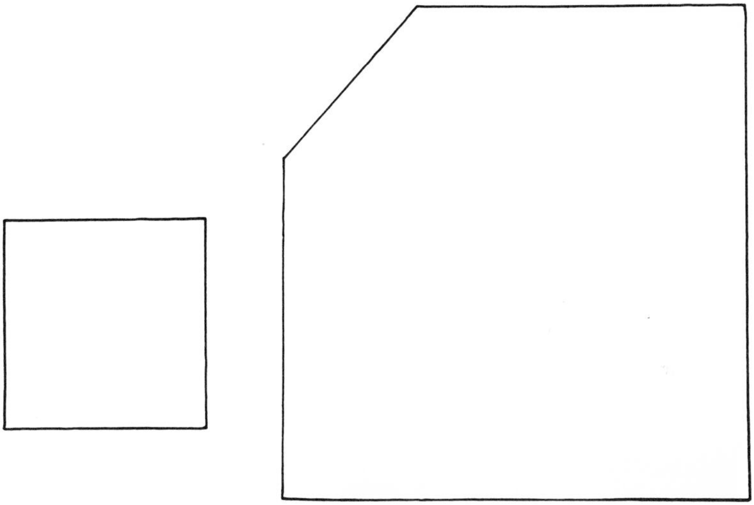

tions or yardage requirements are not given. If you do want to purchase special fabric for the pattern, follow this simple estimating method: decide what size you would like your individual squares to be, then figure how many you will need to make the quilt its finished size. Then, estimate how many of these blocks you can cut from $\frac{1}{2}$ yard of material and buy your material to equal all the blocks you need.

With right sides together, piece the three sections together that form the bow-tie, and then piece the other two blocks to the tie. With white thread (unless you are using very dark material) sew the blocks together with $\frac{1}{4}$-inch seams. These blocks are not usually set together with strips, but if you would like to do so, simply figure the width and length of each strip and sew the strips with a $\frac{1}{4}$-inch stitch to the bow-tie blocks.

Illus. 25. This is the Lone Star Quilt whose directions begin on page 23.

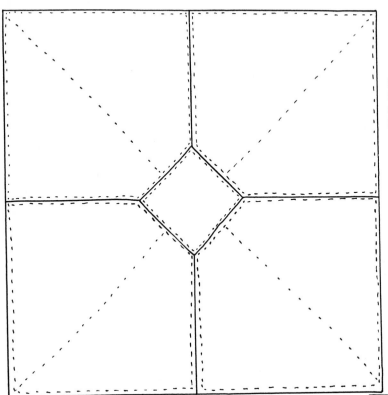

Illus. 26. Suggested quilting lines for the Bow-Tie Quilt. (Throughout this book, straight broken lines indicate quilting lines.)

Quilt along the edge of each piece so the bow-tie pattern is reversed on the quilt back. Or, see the quilting suggestion in Illus. 27 for another possible pattern for the quilting lines.

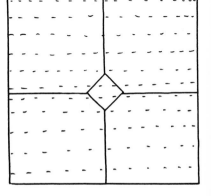

Illus. 27. Another possible quilting pattern for the Bow-Tie Quilt.

Lone Star Quilt

One of the most popular of all American motifs in quilt patterns is the star, of which there are more than 100 pattern variations. A very common pattern is the Lone Star Quilt, known in some areas as the Rising Sun and Star of the West. Whichever of these names you have heard, the pattern is probably the same: small diamonds pieced together to make eight identical sections which are joined for the large eight-point star. In addition to the large middle star, many Lone Star quilts have smaller stars and half stars appliquéd to the background. The Lone Star is classified as a masterpiece quilt because it is intricate, but if you cut your pattern carefully and sew evenly you should have no trouble piecing this beautiful quilt.

First select colors for the quilt. Lay all colors out in some pattern and notice their over-all effect. Experiment with new and bold colors and try some new combinations. Lavender and yellow make a lovely combination, as do orange and blue in subtle tones. This pattern is basically the same in all designs and if you find a particular color combination you prefer, simply use this diamond pattern and follow the general directions to make your pattern.

Because the finished size of this quilt depends on the size border you use in the pattern, you can make the completed quilt larger or smaller than the suggested finished size. If you follow the diamond pattern in Illus. 28 and add a border of $5\frac{3}{4}$ inches on the sides and 8 inches on the top and bottom, the finished quilt should be approximately 87 inches long and 77 inches wide. However, by adding more diamonds in the piecing order given, or by adding a wider border, you can enlarge the quilt. To make a smaller quilt, simply use a smaller diamond pattern.

To make the quilt shown in Illus. 25, you need the following material: $\frac{1}{4}$ yard of dark purple for the 8 middle diamonds; $\frac{1}{2}$ yard or less each, depending on the width of material, for the 16 medium purple and for the 24 light purple diamonds; $1\frac{1}{2}$ yards of material for the 72 dark pink diamonds; 1 yard of red for the 48 red diamonds; 1 yard each of medium pink and light pink; $\frac{1}{2}$ yard of yellow and light green, and $\frac{1}{4}$ yard of dark green.

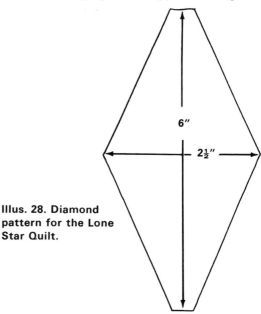

Illus. 28. Diamond pattern for the Lone Star Quilt.

6"

2½"

Illus. 29. A baby quilt is a wonderful gift for any newborn child. Because the size is often relatively small, you can design and create a baby quilt faster than most full-sized quilts.

Illus. 30. Many simple, but decorative, motifs make charming appliqués. This señorita, appliquéd to a complementary background, is a lively figure to adorn a quilt.

Illus. 31. This is another possible cradle quilt you can make.

Illus. 32. Flowers lend themselves well to appliquéd quilts. This is a dahlia, but you can choose any flower you like.

Illus. 33. Appliqués need not be exact imitations of natural colors. These patterned butterflies certainly are not true-to-life, but are, nevertheless, attractive motifs for a quilt.

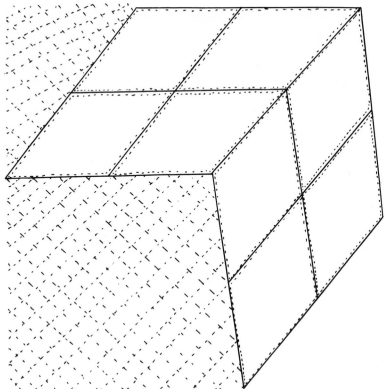

Cut 40 medium pink diamonds, 32 light pink, 24 yellow, 16 light green and 8 dark green.

The star consists of eight diamond-shaped sections, each section a parallelogram with six rows of six diamonds. To make the first star section, piece diamonds together in the following order: dark purple, medium purple, light purple, two rows of dark pink, red. Piece the second row starting with medium purple and ending with medium pink. Begin the third row with light purple and end with light pink. Continue piecing in this manner until you have pieced all six rows. Sew the rows together to form a parallelogram.

When you have completed the first section, make seven more following the same directions. Having all dark purple points in the center, join four sections to make half of the star and then the other four sections for the other half. Join the two halves to finish the eight-point star.

After completing the star, measure the distance

between the points on the star and cut six squares of background material (you will need four or five yards of this background material) to fit into the corner squares on the star. Cut two of the squares in half diagonally so you have four triangles. Sew the squares and triangles to the star as shown in Illus. 25.

Using any color scrap material left from the large star, cut enough diamonds to make four whole stars and four half stars. Sew the diamonds together and turn the small star edges under. Appliqué the whole stars to the squares and the half stars to the triangles as shown in Illus. 25. (See page 33 for instructions on the appliqué stitches.)

You need approximately $7\frac{1}{2}$ yards of material for the backing and the border of the quilt. In the photograph of the Lone Star, the backing material is white, as is the filler between star points, and the border is the yellow in the large star. You may, however, use a print material for the back and a solid from the star for the border. A border 8 to 10 inches wide would look nice on this quilt, but you may use a larger border to increase the quilt size. Cut four border strips, piece them together and stitch them around the top of the quilt using $\frac{1}{4}$-inch seams.

The Lone Star quilt is usually quilted according to the pattern in Illus. 34. However, you can choose any quilting pattern you want for the border. It is recommended that the thread for the quilting match the backing material.

Illus. 35. Suggested quilting pattern for the border of the Lone Star Quilt.

Illus. 36. This Rose Quilt is a lovely addition in any bedroom, living room or den. The design is simple, but the effect striking if you choose attractive colors. Refer to pages 40 and 41 for instructions and patterns.

Illus. 37. Overall Sam is a fun quilt to design, because you have unlimited choice in dressing him. You can use different scraps for the overalls and shirt of each figure on the quilt. See pages 38 and 39 for instructions and patterns.

Grandmother's Flower Garden Quilt

Often, quilts can serve as remembrances of special events or motifs. A century and more ago, Presentation quilts were very popular. Women of the community worked on individual blocks, pieced and quilted them and then presented the quilt to a special friend or, more commonly, to a visiting dignitary.

Like many other quilts, this one is known by several names—Martha Washington's Garden, The Mosaic, The Hexagon, or The Honeycomb. The important difference when it is called a "garden" quilt, whether it is Martha Washington's or Grandmother's, is that each flower is surrounded by a row of green to represent flower leaves and then a row of white to represent the winding path through the garden.

Grandmother's Flower Garden Quilt is a beautiful quilt and is considered, by many, a treasure to own. It is a difficult quilt to piece and you must do it with care and precision. When you have finished, however, you will certainly consider it one of the best quilts in your collection.

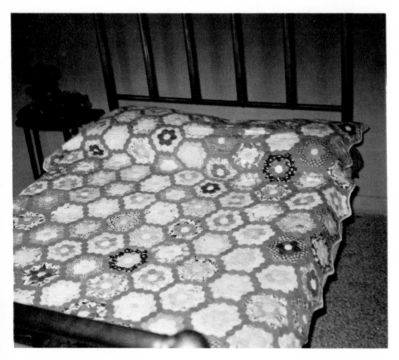

Illus. 38. Usually Grandmother's Flower Garden Quilt has a definite order of colors. Although this variation does follow the traditional pattern, however, the colors are totally different. You can, of course, choose any colors to suit your particular needs and taste.

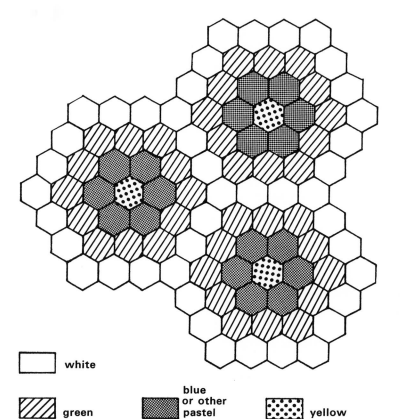

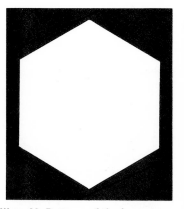

☐ white

▨ green

▦ blue or other pastel

▨ yellow

Illus. 40. Pattern of the hexagon.

You make the entire quilt cover of small hexagons, six-sided patches, sewn together to resemble flowers. If you wish to make the quilt a true flower garden, cut the center hexagon of each block from yellow material, the next row from pink, blue, or another pastel material, the third row (the foliage row) from green and the connecting row from white. It is extremely important that you cut all pieces accurately so that all the edges are sharp.

To figure the amount of material you need for each color, decide how large you want the finished quilt to be; then, measure the hexagon and see how many will fit into $\frac{1}{2}$ yard of material. Estimate how many hexagons you need for the entire quilt and divide this total by the number you need of each color.

When you have cut the hexagons, select the middle hexagon and sew the second row to this middle piece, making a $\frac{1}{4}$-inch seam all round.

Next, sew the hexagons together with the same size seams. Continue adding row by row, sewing first the edges of the preceding row and then sewing the new row together. When you are ready to sew the path row or white row together, you have to join the flower blocks. See Illus. 39. Be sure that all the seams are straight and even.

When you have finished piecing this quilt, it will have a naturally scalloped border. Instead of turning the edge under and hemming it, sew bias tape round the edge to finish it off. If you only want the ends of the quilt scalloped, or only the edges, follow Illus. 42. Only piece part of the flower pattern, as shown in Illus. 42, instead of the full flower along the edges you want to be even. When you have completed this piecing, the edges of the quilt have small points, as shown. Cut these points off following the dotted line in Illus. 42. Then, finish the edge with bias tape or quilt binding.

To quilt, follow the seam lines around each hexagon, as shown in Illus. 41. Do not quilt through the middle of any patch.

This quilt is often made as a coverlet or bedspread with a dust ruffle added in a matching color.

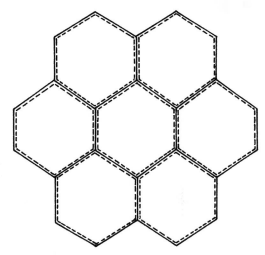

Illus. 41 (above). Suggested quilting lines for Grandmother's Flower Garden Quilt.

Illus. 42 (below). To scallop the edges, only piece part of the outside flower section as shown.

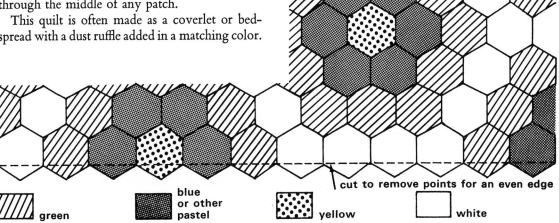

cut to remove points for an even edge

green   blue or other pastel   yellow   white

31

Illus. 43. This is a simple baby quilt appliquéd with randomly placed, multi-colored tulips.

Illus. 44. Fairy tales and nursery rhymes, such as Humpty Dumpty, are appropriate inspirations for children's quilts.

Appliquéd Quilts

Many beginning quilters shy away from appliqué patterns thinking they are too difficult or time consuming when quite the contrary is true. Appliqué quilts demand more skill in hand-sewing, but are often simpler and quicker to make than intricate patchwork. An appliquéd quilt is sometimes referred to as a "laid-on" quilt because you cut the pieces of the design out of different materials and lay them on or appliqué them to a plain background. You use a hemming stitch, slip stitch or buttonhole stitch to hold these pieces in place.

You must take great care when making an appliqué quilt to cut the pieces carefully and to allow $\frac{1}{4}$ inch on the pattern pieces for turning edges. As you cut the pieces, keep them in order by stringing them as you did for patchwork. Press all the pieces. Then, turn down the edges of each piece $\frac{1}{4}$ inch and crease them in place with your thumb and forefinger. If you do not turn under and stitch the pieces, they often pull out and the edges fray badly. You may have to make small cuts or notches $\frac{1}{8}$ inch deep in corners or sharp turns to maintain the outline of your pattern.

Baste these turned-down edges with a long running stitch. Since you will remove these basting threads, for identification use a contrasting thread color and keep your knot on the top of the piece. When you have turned and basted all the pieces, press them again with a warm iron. Now you are ready to assemble the over-all design you have chosen for each individual block or quilt top. Once you have set your pieces in place, hold them securely with a long basting stitch.

Appliqué Stitches

You can work the actual appliqué stitch in black embroidery thread, for an outline stitch, or a color to match the appliquéd piece for a less obvious stitch. Six-strand cotton embroidery floss works best for appliqué stitches, as you can use all six strands or less, if you separate the threads.

Just as your pattern design determines the quilting stitch you use, so it determines the appliqué stitch you use. Use the hemming stitch or slip stitch (Illus. 46) when you are sewing flowers or other delicate pattern pieces to the quilt top. Use the buttonhole stitch (Illus. 47), probably the most common appliqué stitch, to emphasize a particular part of a design or when each block contains one figure or motif, such as the tulip (see page 36) or sunbonnet girl (see page 38).

Illus. 45. This is the traditional bridal quilt pattern. Notice the lovely simplicity produced by hearts and leaves.

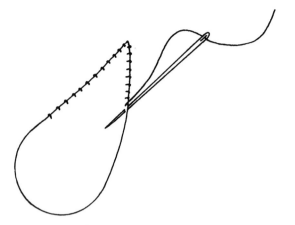

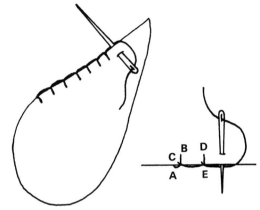

Illus. 46. Use the slip stitch for appliqué work in which you do not need to emphasize the outline of the design.

Illus. 47. Use the buttonhole stitch to emphasize a particular appliqué pattern piece. Follow the steps in the drawing on the right.

This buttonhole stitch not only produces a bold outline for appliqué pattern pieces that you want to emphasize, but it also holds the piece securely. It will not hold the edges, however, unless the stitches are close to each other. For this reason, when you use the buttonhole stitch, use a fine running stitch round the edges of the pattern piece to hold turned edges under and then do the buttonhole stitch over this. This way, when you pull the basting threads out, the material edges will not come out too. To make the buttonhole stitch, begin at the left and sew towards the right, looping the thread below the needle on each stitch (see Illus. 47). Finish thread strands off with a backstitch and a fine knot on the back of the appliqué piece.

Another appliqué stitch is a simple slip stitch for which you alternate long and short stitches, making a decorative and fine, delicate stitch. To make this stitch, bring the needle out on the inside edge of the pattern piece, go in on the background block, and come out again on the inside edge of the pattern piece (see Illus. 48).

Use an appliqué stitch much like the hemming stitch for work that does not require an outline emphasis. Sewing right to left, catch the folded edge of the appliqué piece to the background material. Take stitches less than $\frac{1}{8}$ inch long, so the thread on the top of the pattern piece shows as little as possible.

Many of the new model sewing machines are equipped to do various outline or zig-zag stitches, several of which are suited for machine appliqué work. The machine zig-zag or satin stitch makes a neat appliqué outline and holds an appliqué design better than a loose hand stitch. In fact, if you work the machine stitches close to each other, depending on the material, you may not have to turn the edges on the appliqué pieces. If the material seems to have a tendency to fray, however, it is better to turn the edges. If you choose to

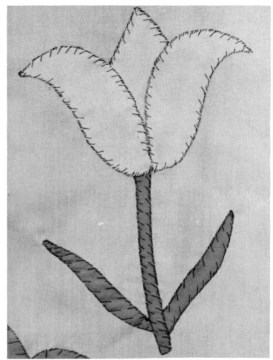

machine-stitch your design, experiment with the correct stitch length and width and the proper tension for your machine before beginning your actual quilt.

As with the patchwork quilt, if you are a beginning quilter, you would be wise to choose a simple pattern for your first appliqué quilt and then proceed to patterns with more intricate parts.

Illus. 49. The appliqué on this bridal quilt consists of machine-sewn zig-zag stitches.

Tulip Quilt

The Tulip Quilt is one of many quilts with flower patterns and this particular tulip is one of many tulip variations. This quilt is versatile and easy to piece for anyone regardless of past quilting experience. Because you frame each tulip in its own block, you can use any color combinations and the quilt can be either a spring-time color assortment or a one-color garden.

The recommended size for blocks for this quilt is approximately 14 × 16 inches which allows more room for the height of the flowers and

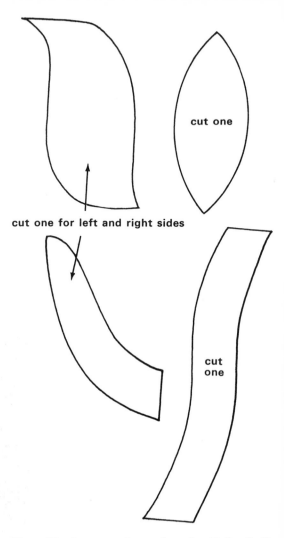

cut one

cut one for left and right sides

cut one

Illus. 51. Pattern pieces for the Tulip Quilt.

Illus. 50. An intricate motif is not necessary for an attractive quilt. These colorful but simple tulips are easy to piece.

36

gives each flower a block large enough to show it off. Usually, the tulips are pieced from solid material—any color for the flower and some shade of green for the stem and leaves. Cut all pattern pieces, according to the pattern in Illus. 51, from whatever colors you have chosen and turn the edges as directed on page 32.

Baste, then appliqué all flowers to the blocks (see Illus. 52). Set the quilt together with strips of material chosen to match either the flower petals or the green in the leaves.

Quilt this pattern around the edges of each flower petal and around the stem and leaves. If there is a blank space more than 3 inches within the flower block, quilt a small flower or other design in each corner so that the filling will not shift or bunch when you launder the quilt.

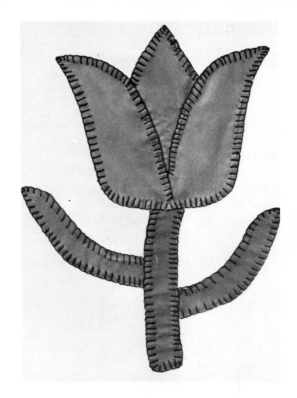

Illus. 52. Close-up of the appliqué stitches on the tulip.

Sunbonnet Sue
and Overall Sam

Sunbonnet Sue (see back cover) and her friend Overall Sam (see Illus. 37) can be found in many different poses on quilt tops everywhere. These two charming figures seem to be most popular for grandmothers to make for their grandchildren. Many little girls have a Sunbonnet Sue dressed in

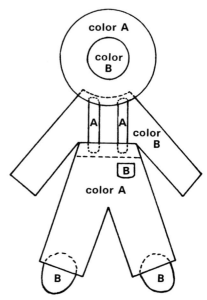

Illus. 54. Pattern for Overall Sam.

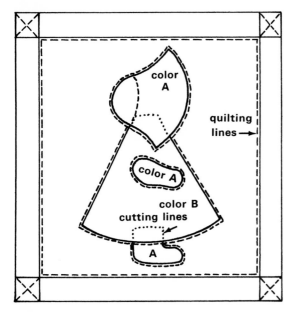

Illus. 53. Cut Sunbonnet Sue along the solid lines, following the dotted lines for the shoes and bodice top. You may follow the straight broken lines for quilting.

all the same dresses she has. What a nice way for a little girl to remember her childhood days.

For these patterns, appliqué either the boy or girl figure or both onto a white background block. Use small prints for the dresses and shirts and solids for the pants and hats.

Overall Sam is simple to make and you can sew him as elaborately or as simply as you desire. Although in Illus. 37, Sam is not wearing blue denim overalls, he can be a real farm hand with blue denim overalls and a sun hat. If you cannot get soft blue denim, use brown, navy blue, or any dark-colored cotton you wish. Often, Sam is combined in a quilt with Sunbonnet Sue and his shirt is made from the same material as her dress.

Blocks for this quilt can be as large as 15 inches square or as small as 8 inches square. Simply draw your pattern figure to fit whichever size block you use, leaving some border space within the block on all sides. See Illus. 53 and 54 for the patterns. Cut all pattern pieces, prepare and baste them according to the directions in the appliqué section on page 32. Make sure you cut Sam's suspenders (braces) long enough to tuck under his hat and pants.

Stitch all pieces onto the blocks. When you have appliquéd all the blocks, you can set the quilt together. At this time, if you wish to personalize the quilt, you can put balloons in the girl's hand or embroider flowers round the band of her hat. Add a pocket to Sam's pants, if you

want, or, to make him an authentic farm boy, place a small, cloth triangle handkerchief inside the pocket of his shirt. For a real blue-jean look, you can top-stitch with white thread round the edges of his pants. Additional embroidery you can add to Sam's block includes a fishing pole and bucket, a dog or cat, or a hoe and shovel.

Quilt Sunbonnet Sue around the edge of the figure and around her arm and the entire hat (see Illus. 53). Quilt Sam, like Sue, around the outline of the figure and then around the hat, inside rim and center circle, then along the suspenders and pants top.

If you make larger figures, quilt through the band of both hats and across the top of Sam's pants.

Illus. 55. Close-up of Sunbonnet Sue. Add flowers, if you wish, for an individual touch.

Illus. 56. Close-up of Overall Sam. Notice the machine-sewn zig-zag appliqué stitches.

Rose Quilt

Like the Tulip, the Rose Quilt has many pattern variations. Most patterns following this basic design are referred to as Rose of Sharon quilts. Color selections and border designs seem to determine whether or not the quilt is called Rose of Sharon. The woman who made the quilt described here simply calls hers the Rose Quilt.

This pattern consists of one large flower with a smaller center surrounded by four buds or flowers and a circle of foliage. The quilt looks quite nice as a two-color pattern, using light and dark shades of the same color for the flower and buds, and green for the stems and leaves. You can set the quilt together with one of the flower colors.

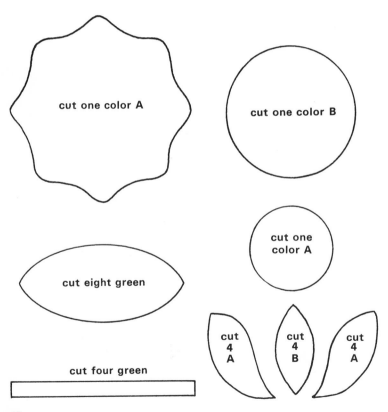

cut one color A

cut one color B

cut one color A

cut eight green

cut four green

cut 4 A

cut 4 B

cut 4 A

Illus. 57. Pattern pieces for the Rose Quilt. The actual size you cut the roses depends on the size you want the finished quilt to be.

Illus. 58. Suggested quilting pattern for the Rose Quilt.

Blocks for this quilt can be from 15 to 20 inches square. If you would like a different effect, appliqué the flower arrangement directly onto a solid quilt top eliminating the use of blocks.

Cut all necessary pattern pieces in the colors you have selected (see Illus. 57), turn the edges under and baste. Place the cut-out pieces on the quilt block and slip the stems under the large flower and under the smaller buds so the ends do not show. When you have placed all the stems, baste the pieces down and appliqué the flowers in place. Sew the leaves on the quilt last, so that you can center them between the extended buds.

When you have completed the blocks, piece them with strips and set the quilt together. Quilting directions for this quilt are like those for most appliqué quilts: follow the lines of the pattern and quilt around each separate pattern piece (see Illus. 58). A border is not called for in this pattern and is, therefore, optional. However, if you do choose to put a large border on the quilt, consider decorating it with the same flower you placed in the center of the block. Such a border is often added to this quilt.

Illus. 36 shows this Rose Quilt in color.

Baby Quilts

Baby quilts are something special. They seem to carry more love in each piece than any quilt four times their size, and what a lovely addition to any newborn's layette! Baby quilts, because of their size, are so simple to make that every baby might have one made by a mother, grandmother or family friend.

If you have been hesitant to begin a full-sized quilt, what better way to try a pattern than in miniature? Infant quilts offer an excellent opportunity for the quilter anxious to design a new pattern to start on a small scale. You can make baby quilts from any pattern you like, but there are a few patterns especially suitable for infant quilts. Animals, small block designs, nursery-rhyme figures and pastel flower bouquets are popular motifs for baby quilts.

You must be more selective than usual in choosing material for a baby quilt, however. Remember that even though most quilts will not be next to or touch the baby's skin, the fabric should be soft and easily washable, just in case. Always pre-wash material for an infant quilt to remove excessive dyes and soften the material.

When choosing a filling for your baby quilt, keep in mind that you will probably launder the quilt frequently. The new dacron (terylene) and polyester fillings are light and fluffy and launder beautifully.

Baby quilts may vary in size from 36 × 36 to 45 inches square or larger. The size of the quilt depends on the pattern you select and on the type of quilt you are making. A throw quilt need not be as large as a quilt to be used for a crib blanket, and a quilt or coverlet designed for a cradle or carriage can be smaller than a crib quilt.

Infant quilts are easy to machine-quilt because of their small size. Also, some need not be put into a frame to be quilted, and you can simply baste them securely around the edges and through the middle with a large X.

Although you usually hem quilts with an overlap of the backing material, infant quilts seem to have more of a finished look when you place binding round the edges. Binding is inexpensive and easy to use. Follow the directions on the binding package or the steps in Illus. 8 to 10 on page 11 to 12.

Teddy Bear Quilt

This Teddy Bear Quilt was designed by the author as her little girl's first quilt. It makes a wonderful homecoming present for any new mother and baby. The center square (see Illus. 60) is reserved for the baby's name, birth date, and any other special information you might want to add. Because the bear figures are one simple

Illus. 59. Pattern for the teddy bear.

Illus. 60. Reserve the middle square for the baby's name and birthdate or any other embroidery or appliqué you want.

pattern (see Illus. 59), this quilt is easy and fun to make.

Since the size of the quilt depends on how you plan to use it, specific size requirements are not given, just general directions for assembly and quilting. In the pictured quilt, the bears are appliquéd onto individual blocks, then set together with strips of material with small connecting blocks. The strips match the material chosen for the quilt back. You could, however, place the bears on one solid piece of material and leave an open space in the middle of the quilt to embroider the child's name.

After you have attached the bears to the blocks, using a hand appliqué or machine zig-zag stitch,

Illus. 61. Close-up of the teddy bear. Note the touch the embroidered butterfly adds.

Humpty Dumpty Quilt

The Humpty Dumpty Quilt, designed from the famous nursery story of the same name, makes a decorative quilt or a charming wall hanging for a child's room. The figures on the quilt are large and bold and take up most of the quilt top space, so there is no need for an elaborate design.

The quilt in Illus. 44 was made from fuzzy cotton knit pieces, sewn to the quilt top with a zig-zag appliqué stitch. The smaller background pieces (the bricks) were placed on first, then Humpty Dumpty was set on the brick wall. You can sew additional figures to the quilt pattern and you can scale the quilt to any desired size. Although this quilt was machine appliquéd, it was hand-quilted around Humpty Dumpty and the smaller pieces. The remainder of the quilt was quilted in straight lines, approximately 2 inches apart, from top to bottom.

Humpty Dumpty is just one example of making a quilt from a popular children's story or poem. Children identify with and remember the story that goes with them. Do not forget all the quilting possibilities in other popular nursery rhymes and story books.

embroider eyes, nose, mouth and paws. You can embroider the information about the child at this time or after you have assembled the quilt. Because this pattern is so simple, embroidery changes the appearance of each quilt. You can embroider delicate flowers, birds or any other design to give your quilt a very personal touch.

Quilt around the outside edge of each bear, and along the seam lines of the separating strips. Small quilted flowers or a scroll design will fill the center block very well.

Teddy bears seem to be popular with children of all ages. To enlarge this quilt for use by an older child, either make larger teddy bears or simply cut more of them.

Tacked Quilts

Tacked or tied quilts are just what their name implies. Instead of using quilting stitches to hold the three quilt layers together, you tie yarn or crochet thread in double knots, at intervals, through all three layers, as was done in early colonial quilts. Tacked quilts are just as sturdy as quilted ones, and much faster to make, but you must space the knots or tacked points fairly close together.

Most tacked quilts are square patch quilts with knots tied in the corners and in the middle of each block. You can adapt almost any pattern to a

tacked design, if you work out an attractive pattern for tying the knots.

To tack your quilt, thread a large-eyed needle with heavy crochet thread or knitting worsted. Using the thread double, push the needle from the top through all three quilt layers, leaving the thread end on top. Push the needle up from the bottom of the quilt about $\frac{1}{2}$ inch away from the first thread. Tie the thread in a firm double knot and clip the ends of the thread, leaving at least $\frac{1}{2}$ inch.

You can use cotton or dacron (terylene) filling

Illus. 62. Instead of quilting, you may tack a quilt by tying knots either in the corners and middle of your patched squares, as shown here, or in any decorative pattern you design.

in tacked quilts. Many quilters use new light-weight acrylic blankets between the quilt layers for an extra heavy quilt, or a sheet for a light-weight quilt. You can use heavier materials for making tacked quilts than those you use for quilted ones. Many beautiful tacked quilts are even made from wool pieces. There certainly could be no warmer blanket on a cold winter night.

If you enjoy patchwork, piece a quilt and invite your friends to a tacking party. There is no need to put a tacked quilt in a frame, if you baste it securely, and then anyone can come and help you tie a few knots here and there.

Design Your Own Quilts

When our great-grandmothers made quilts, they relied on their own imaginations for quilt designs, and everything around them became a potential pattern. Trees and leaves, a garden trellis, a water pump, flowers, and garden plants inspired the patterns still used in quilting today. Too often, however, quilters rely entirely on standard patterns and are at a loss for making their own designs.

Even if you have an urge to create an individual pattern, you may not know where to begin. You start drawing in some hodge-podge fashion and end up nowhere. Before you become discouraged, take a hint from earlier quilters—often the simplest natural things make the most beautiful patterns. Look closely at flowers or leaves, find the design in a seashell, see how honeysuckle vines climb, look at birds silhouetted against the sky. If you live in the city, look at windows in a large office building, find a pattern in buildings lining the street, catch a glimpse of a large bridge from a new angle, or look at the pattern streets make on a city map.

There is, in addition, a new trend in quilt-making. Quilters today are not making quilts out of necessity for warmth, but rather as a means of self expression and as a chance to make something with their hands. With this new interest in quilting, quilts are no longer confined to use as bedcovers. Now, they decorate walls, floors and furniture, and, with a slight sizing variation, appear at parties as women's skirts and capes. Needless to say, with these new uses for quilts, come new and bolder designs. Quilts are covered with faces taken from photographs, full-sized bodies reclining, and abstract figures running and dancing. New symbols of the times are popular themes for quilts—the ecology movements, the peace dove and space flights.

This trend of using the quilt as a means of art expression is not really new, although early quilters may not have been aware of the master-pieces they were creating. While some quilters just did what came natural and followed their eye for color, they created some thoroughly modern geometric patterns on their quilt tops which are now hanging in craft museums. Quilt-ing is not new and certainly beautiful patterns are not new. There are just a lot of people dis-covering the world of quilting for the first time.

Simply making a quilt is a very rewarding thing —you will have a special pride in seeing your own handiwork, especially in something people will use. You can feel even more satisfied when the quilt is your own unique design. After you know the basics of putting a quilt together, experiment with new and different designs. Let the next quilt you make really be a part of you.

Index